# FUNDED andFREE

**FUND your church
and FREE yourself
from financial worry!**

## CASEY GRAHAM

## JOSEPH SANGL

NIN Publishing

Cover design by Chris Dunagan

Library of Congress Control Number: 2010907147

Sangl, Joseph; Graham, Casey

ISBN 978-1-4507-1763-2

First Edition

Printed in the United States by Morris Publishing®
3212 East Highway 30
Kearney, NE 68847
1-800-650-7888

I dedicate this book to my wife, Kacie.
Thank you for always believing in me.
– Casey


For my bride, Jennifer, daughter, Melea, and
son, Keaton. You are my pride and joy!
– Joe


And to all of the church leaders we have been
given the privilege of serving.

# CONTENTS

# Contents

## Contents

# • Introduction •

This book is for every church leader looking to generate more money for ministry.

One of the top issues faced by leaders is the challenge of increasing operational income. Most of us know how to accurately account for money, but it is difficult for many to generate additional revenue. Yet in formal education, this topic is rarely or barely addressed. It is essential that leaders equip themselves to address this vital component to the long-term success of their ministry.

We have heard it said that pastors must equip their congregation financially because they want something FOR them instead of FROM them. That is what this book is all about. It has been written to equip leaders to fund the vision of their church with proven principles and steps that can be read today and implemented immediately. These are not gimmicks or tricks. These are proven biblical financial management principles and funding techniques.

This book is a collection of practices we have observed through our own experiences and the experiences of the churches we have worked with. It is our hope that a church leader can pick up this book, turn to any page and read information that will immediately help them fund the Kingdom even more. We pray that as you apply the principles and techniques in this book, you will see even more funding for the vision God has given you.

For more discussion and to obtain additional resources, visit www.FundedAndFree.com.

# GET FIRED UP!

*Understand 5 Reasons People Give*

To fund the vision God has given you for your church, it is important to understand why people give. We have found that there are five basic reasons that an individual will give money to an organization.

## 1. Relationship

People will give money to a larger organization because of the relationship they have with the people there. If a person participates in a small group and are connected with many relationships at your church because they volunteer regularly, they are much more likely to give money to the church because it is impacting them relationally.

## 2. Vision

Strong vision inspires people to give. Proverbs 29:18 (KJV) states: "without vision, the people perish." Clear vision helps people understand the key next steps that God wants for your church and connects them to the amount of money it will take to be well-funded.

Be careful, however, because too often leaders are told that people give to vision and vision alone. Vision is vital, but it is not the only reason people give.

## 3. Need

We have heard it said that "people give to vision, not to need." This is simply not the case! When the enormous tsunami struck Indonesia, Sri Lanka, India, and several other nations on December 26, 2004 and killed 250,000 people, the outpouring of giving was unprecedented. When Port-Au-Prince, Haiti collapsed in an earthquake on January 12, 2010, people gave in an incredible way!

People will give to need. Express a need clearly and show them how addressing it will help the church accomplish its mission. People will give.

## 4. Obedience

Many people give because they are living lives that are obedient to God's Word. They understand that God is an incredible giver (He gave His only Son!), and they are grateful to have been blessed with some money. You can build a city-shaking, life-impacting ministry when you have a group of people living their lives in obedience in this way!

## 5. Education

People give because they have been educated about what God's Word says about money, and they have been taught practical tools that helped them put their desire to give into action.

The vast majority of people want to give, but sadly, many people have not been taught how to manage their money well. As a result, they have pledged away all of their money (or maybe a little more) to the lender. It is important to educate people on God's principles of money management and to teach practical ways to put Scriptures regarding money into practice.

Ask people in your church the question, "Why do you give?"

# • 2 •

## *Margin. Margin. Margin.*

If the vision is to have a sustainable ministry, there must be financial margin. The economy will go up and down. This means that giving will go up and down. If the bank account is perpetually empty, the church will immediately experience financial hardship when giving decreases. Poor economic times are extremely important times for ministry to take place. This is impossible if there is no financial margin.

In Genesis 41, Joseph interpreted a dream God had given to Pharaoh. He saw that there would be seven years of plenty followed by seven years of famine. Joseph not only interpreted the dream, but provided a plan to Pharaoh that would allow Egypt to survive and prosper during the famine. Joseph told Pharaoh that they were to save 20 percent of their production for each of the next seven years so that they could cover the time of famine. Margin. Pharaoh put Joseph in charge of the plan. He executed the plan, everyone saved, and the country prospered in spite of the bad times.

It is certainly exciting to spend the entire bank account on a particular program or event, but it is not wise unless God has specifically told you to do so. It is very rare that God commands a church to spend all of its resources and maintain a zero balance. Proverbs 21:20 speaks to the importance of establishing and maintaining margin, *"In the house of the wise are stores of choice food and oil, but a foolish man devours all he has."*

If your giving dropped 30 percent today, how long would your ministry be able to sustain itself? If the answer is less than six months, you do not have a sustainable ministry.

Financial margin allows you to have financial confidence to take risks and to fund the vision God has given you. It also allows you to remain focused on the vision even when the largest giver in the church attempts to distract you from it.

# • 3 •

## *Create An Obstacle And Opportunity Fund*

Your church will face obstacles. Technology breaks, people sue, leaders have moral failures, taxes don't get paid, church buildings burn and wear out, and crazy stuff just happens. All of the surprise stuff shouldn't be surprising! It IS going to happen.

Your church will face opportunities. A new building will open that you want to move in to, an opportunity to go multi-site will drop in your lap, a person you've been wanting to hire will become available, or a great deal on a piece of technology will appear out of nowhere. Terrific opportunities will arrive on your doorstep. Is your church financially ready?

The churches that are prepared will succeed. The churches that aren't will learn very hard lessons. Prepare by creating an obstacle and opportunity fund (O & O fund).

This reserve is funded with cash that you can access quickly. There should never be less than six weeks of operating budget in the bank. If your weekly budgeted need is $10,000, your O & O fund should always have at least $60,000.

How do you fund your O & O quickly if you currently don't have it? Ask your people to give toward it during a series on finances. Ask them to bring the offering on one day to help the church reach its goal. This fund relieves stress and helps you reach more people for Jesus when opportunities are funded!

### Change Up The Offering

Each year your church has 52 unique opportunities to inspire and educate people on giving. Offering times should be thought through and planned as much as the sermon, music and videos. Seek creative ways to take up the offering so that it can be consistently changed up. This helps keep people engaged in generosity. Giving is truly a time of worship!

Some great ways to energize your offering moments include:

**Mission Moments**

A mission moment is created when you place the mission and vision of your church on the screen for people to read and then celebrate how it is being accomplished. Read stories that were sent to the church via the website. Celebrate ministry areas like student ministry immediately after camp. Show pictures of what happened and talk about how the money the congregation has given has funded that ministry.

**God's Heart**

Use scriptures that share God's heart for us related to giving. We recently took a poll via Twitter and asked, "Why do you give?" Most people replied that they give out of obedience to God. Many new churches have missed this side of giving. It isn't only about our vision for the church. It is about God's heart.

**Personal Story**

Ask someone who has just started giving to share their experience via video. This will inspire new givers to jump in with them. God's Word is true, and many givers will welcome the opportunity to share how God has worked in their life as a result of their investments into God's Kingdom.

**Show them HOW to give**

Use the offering time to show the variety of ways they can give. If you have online giving, walk them through the website and the steps necessary to give online. The same applies for each manner of giving whether it is giving kiosks, checks, cash, automatic withdrawals, or text-messages.

Each year, you have at least 52 opportunities to celebrate the offering. What do you need to do to maximize them?

# • 5 •

*Staff Must Give*

If you are teaching your church community what God's Word says about giving, it is clear that we are to bring at least a tithe of our income to the local church.

Scripture tells us that "where your treasure is, there your heart will be also." Like it or not, ministry happens through financial gifts. The old question and answer is true, "How much ministry can you do for $100?" The answer remains the same: "One hundred dollars worth."

As a leader, you should know if your staff is giving to the ministry. If your staff is not giving, it is impossible to teach the entire church that the staff is 100 percent behind the vision God has given you. If a staff member is not joyfully giving, they need to begin giving or resign. This can be addressed from the beginning by never hiring someone who is not already a generous giver.

When an entire staff is giving generously to the ministry, it unites their hearts toward the God-given vision. It also allows every single staff member to speak with strong authority about the power of giving, and how it has impacted their own lives.

# • 6 •

## *Check Staff Giving*

When consulting with churches, we are stunned to hear a senior pastor state that he believes that all of the staff/team are giving back to the church consistently. There is an easy way to know for sure – check the staff giving records. Some people may believe that this is not the right thing to do, but experience has led us to believe that many staff members do not give back to the church where they serve. This is a big deal! Jesus was clear that we will put our money on what we value.

## 3 Ways to Check Staff Giving In A Healthy Way
### 1. Tell them your expectations

When you hire someone, tell them that you will check their giving records annually. Do NOT assume they will know this expectation. If you haven't told them you are going to do this, set a new expectation for the entire staff in your next staff meeting and tell them you will begin checking giving records in three months.

## 2. Set reminder on your calendar

Set up a reminder in your calendar to check staff giving records on the first week of January. Look for consistent and generous giving. You can't clearly see if the staff's family is giving a tithe but you can certainly tell if the staff member is giving 10 percent.

## 3. Take action

Have a plan prepared for a staff member who is not giving so that you can help them start. Do NOT just beat them up. Listen to them and see what their issue is. You will learn a lot about what has led to the lack of giving from this conversation.

If staff members are giving faithfully, thank them sincerely for their faithfulness. We would suggest giving raises only to people who faithfully give.

# • 7 •

## *Leverage Digital Giving*

Many people will refuse to eat at a restaurant if it does not accept cashless forms of payment. It's really clear to see that we are becoming a cashless society. This means that people who attend our weekend services will not be carrying a bunch of cash or checks with them. In order to maximize the funding for your church's vision, you must have a digital giving strategy for people in your church.

## Two Digital Giving Musts
### 1. Online recurring giving
Have a system connected to your website that allows people to enter their card information in one time and establish recurring gifts. This allows them to "set-it-and-forget-it." This is very convenient and people will be more consistent. In fact, those who give online via established recurring giving are the most consistent givers – their tithe never goes on vacation!

## 2. Giving Kiosks

Again, most people don't have cash on them but just about everyone has a debit or credit card. Giving kiosks in your building are a great way to provide on-ramps for people to give. Please don't use the excuse that you are scared people will give their way into debt. If someone does that and tells you about it, give the money back and teach them how to give consistently using a budget! Have you ever heard someone say, "I gave my way into debt at my church"?

A giving kiosk will pick up more tips than tithes. This is great because it is allowing people to take initial steps toward generous giving. Most of the tithers in your church already have a system that is working for them. The kiosk will give people a great starting point for their journey toward generosity!

## 6 Reasons Why A Church Should Have Giving Kiosks
1. People don't carry a lot of cash.
2. The same reason most people will not eat at a restaurant unless they accept debit or credit cards.
3. MOST places will not accept a personal check in the real world! People carrying checkbooks are limited.
4. It provides a first step for first-time donors and low-budget givers who would usually give nothing.
5. You eliminate another barrier people say prevents giving.
6. It's a very small investment for the return your ministry will receive.

Givers who use digital giving are usually the most consistent donor. You can build an incredible church when you have consistent givers!

# • 8 •

## *Teach Giving*

Scripture asks the question, "How can they hear without someone preaching to them?" (Romans 10:14 NIV) Your church community will learn about the power of giving through your teaching. Tell them the stories of life change that have happened through your church's ministry. Better yet, let people tell their own stories.

The Bible is clear that Christ-followers are to be givers. We are to be known for our giving and compassion for those who are in need. We are to remember the poor. We are to help the poor. We are to reach the world with the life-saving message of Jesus Christ. This is accomplished through financial gifts.

God's Word is full of wisdom about giving. Teach them that God owns it all (Proverbs 24:1-2). Command the rich to give (1 Timothy 6:17). Instruct them about the importance of their giving attitude ("generously" in Romans 12:8; "cheerfully" in 2 Corinthians 9:7).

Tell them how giving has impacted your own life.

Teach about giving regularly – at least four times a year. Do not fear teaching about giving. While many churches have made money the object and have turned a lot of people into skeptics, you are different. You are a person called by God to do His Work. The vision God has given you will happen through people's gifts. Cast vision. Show them how their financial gifts are bringing that God-given vision to reality.

Here are two important questions to ask yourself:
o   How much do you speak about giving at your church?
o   Do you have a hard time speaking about money because you are afraid of offending lost people or the biggest giver in the church?

Do not be intimidated about teaching giving and generosity. God speaks often about the subject. Besides, the vast majority of people who complain about giving messages are the people who are not giving anyway.

# • 9 •

## *Want Something FOR People Instead Of FROM People*

Ask yourself this question – Do you want something FOR people or something FROM people? Andy Stanley once asked this question, and it is a must-ask for every church leader.

The answer must be FOR people. Bill Hybels has stated his belief over and over again that the local church is the hope of the world. We want the life-saving message of Jesus Christ to be proclaimed to all nations. We want to fulfill the Great Commission.

What do you want FOR your people? Jesus focused on meeting physical needs of the hurting. He healed the lame man, the blind man and the dead man. How are you meeting the physical needs of your community?

Are you interested in reaching 500 more people because they will pay for a new building, or are you interested in reaching them because they need Jesus? People know when you are truly interested in them and helping them grow spiritually. They can see insincerity from miles away.

When you adopt a spirit of helping people win with their financial resources using God's Word as the guide so that they can live a more complete life in Christ, your church will become more financially confident. Financial confidence is achieved when people KNOW that you want something FOR them instead of FROM them.

# • 10 •
## *Connect With High Capacity Donors*

One key way to fund the vision for your church is to engage your high-capacity donors. A high-capacity donor is someone who consistently is in the top 5 percent of regular givers in your church. You have to make a decision on how you will approach these people. You can address them in one of three ways.

## 1. Ignore

A lot of pastors choose to ignore this group because they do not want to show favoritism. Ignoring this group of people IS a strategic decision that you make. You are ignoring these people if you don't have a plan to connect with them for any reason. Ignoring high-capacity donors relationally will yield smaller returns.

## 2. Use

It is entirely possible to use your high-capacity donors to fund your vision while not truly caring for them. We see this a lot when a large project is approaching and the pastor begs and pleads for commitments but has done nothing to develop these people long before such a large gift request is made. This creates a "generous when asked" culture. It is obvious when the heart of the leader is more about projects than people.

## 3.  Develop

This is what successful leaders do. They develop the gift of generosity in the lives of their entire church community. It requires an intentional approach toward stewarding the gift of generosity in high-capacity donors. We suggest making this approach as relational as possible. The closer your relationship, the higher the deposit of trust. We trust people that we are close to more than a guy on a stage in a big room.

Here are some key ways you can develop high-capacity donors.

### Meet with them in smaller groups

The smaller the group, the higher the trust. Small groups are best because you can listen to the heart of each person and answer their questions. People love to be heard. This does not mean you must participate in a weekly small group with them, but it is important to create environments where you can gather together several times each year.

### Gather the high-capacity givers together

One thing we know about generous people is they love hearing stories about generosity! After all, they have the spiritual gift of giving! Generosity inspires generosity. Gather people together to share stories at least once a year

### Go to lunch

Have lunch with high-capacity donors regularly. This allows one-on-one conversation and lets you minister to them.

It allows you to connect in a way that will yield great dividends – relationally, spiritually and generously.

Please note that this is a task for the lead pastor. People want to connect with the leader. You can delegate many things, but high-capacity givers respond best when the senior pastor – the one with the direct vision from God – is investing in them.

The bottom line is this – we are all intentionally or unintentionally creating a culture with our top donors. What is your culture?

# • ❚❚ •

## *Cast Clear Vision – Then Do It Again And Again*

We hear a lot of churches say, "We just had Vision Sunday" or our "State of The Church" address. These are good things, but they can't be the only times or ways for vision to be shared. Be sure to use multiple mediums and creative avenues to communicate with your church about why you are doing what you are.

Here are five ways you can cast your vision:

1. **Weekend worship service**

Teach one series a year that clearly outlines the strong vision God has provided and how each person can be a part of it financially. People give to tangible annual goals that are clear!

**2. New member class**

Offer a new member's class and make sure people know what your church is trying to accomplish and how they can be a part of it financially.

### 3. Handwritten notes to first-time givers

Send notes to first-time givers and communicate to them about the vital importance of their giving dollars. Help them understand that their gift is affecting the lives of others in a significant and life-changing manner.

### 4. Quarterly contribution statements

This is a tool for sharing VISION not just information about contributions. Every contribution statement should have a vision letter, a contribution statement and a way to respond (envelope or Web address to online giving).

### 5. Ministry descriptions

Every volunteer role in your church provides people with the opportunity to lead others. Ensure that the volunteer ministry description has clear expectations for them to be faithful and generous in their financial support while serving in this area.

To take a next step in this area, gather a team of people together and ask these questions:
- How can we share the vision of what we are trying to accomplish in three creative ways in the next three months?
- How can we communicate the vision of our church while engaging all five senses?

Vision isn't just a passionate speech, it should permeate everything the church does. So much so that there are clear and subtle reminders of that vision in everything that is done.

# • 12 •

## *Hold Everyone Accountable*

Establish clear and measurable goals and hold everyone accountable. Relentlessly state the vision and the goals necessary to move toward it.

Communicate. Communicate. Communicate. Hold regular goal reviews. Contrary to opinions held by some church leaders, this does not inhibit God's Will. This is ridiculous. Could we really inhibit God's Will? Proverbs 21:5 states that "the plans of the diligent lead to profit."

Develop clear financial goals. Prepare a budget, and hold people accountable to operate within it. The budget is the boss. There is freedom when boundaries are clearly defined.

Everyone must be held accountable. Accountability leads to clarity of the mission. It fosters an environment of open communication. Regular discussion of goals allows you to state the vision again. The vision that God has given you can not be stated often enough! Accountability provides regular feedback to each employee on their performance and the steps they can take to improve.

The most confident employees are those who know the vision and know beyond a shadow of doubt that they are helping the vision become reality.

# • 13 •

## *Involve Others*

The success of your church depends upon your willingness to involve others. As your church accomplishes its mission, it will lead to financial confidence.

The more involved people are with your ministry, the more committed they will be toward the vision. This will lead to more financial investment into the God-ordained work.

Leaders with a strong vision sometimes believe that since they have been given the call, they are the only ones who can make it happen. That is a lie from Satan. You cannot do this by yourself.

Communicate your vision to others. God will send help your way. It will not always be obvious, so be on the lookout for help. It could be a wildly successful business owner who God is telling to sell her business so she can help you accomplish the mission God has given you.

Make the big ask. Ask others to participate. Seek opportunities to cast vision and ask for participation. It bears repeating: you cannot do this alone! To accomplish your vision, you will need someone to answer the phone, clean the building, visit the sick and manage the finances. You will have the joy of doing all of these tasks until you find someone else. If you do not ask others to participate, they will not have the reward of helping you see the vision become reality.

Involve others. There are people ready to help you right now if you would simply ask. Who do you need to ask?

# • 14 •

## *Recognize The Power Of Volunteers*

To accomplish the vision and call that God has placed on your life, you must have help. You cannot do it yourself, and it is easy to attempt to solve the problem by hiring staff.

New staff members cost way more than their salary. They bring additional costs including a new computer, cell phone, insurance and retirement benefits. And they will want space in the budget.

Hiring additional staff can limit the amount of financial resources available to fund ministry. Staff should not be in the business of doing all of the work. They should be focused on *leading* the work through volunteers.

This accomplishes two things. It involves more people in your ministry, and it requires fewer expenditures. Check this out: Volunteers work for FREE and LOVE IT!

Volunteers are a key component to accomplishing your God-given vision. God has chosen to use people. He has chosen you to cast the vision. He has chosen volunteers to make the vision become reality.

When faced with a need for help, always consider using volunteers before hiring additional staff. Volunteers have incredible education and abilities. They are passionate about what God is doing through your church. Many volunteers want to do way more than give money. They want to be the hands and feet that are participating in life-changing work. Volunteers can lead events, call people, develop new ministries, counsel and pray. They can build, advise and listen.  Volunteering is also a great way to have an extended job interview and evaluation period for a potential staff member!

You cannot do all of the work God has called you to do. Your staff cannot do it all either. The accomplishment of the vision God has given you depends on your use of volunteers.

# • 15 •
## *Maximize Capital Campaigns*

Some churches love capital campaigns, some despise them and some never consider them. There is a new philosophy in the fund-raising industry that states, "We should create a culture of generosity versus leading capital campaigns." We do not see it as a clear "either/or" scenario. There are absolutely times when capital campaigns are vital and necessary steps toward funding the vision. In fact, capital campaigns can and should be a time of significant spiritual growth for your church!

We have seen some capital campaigns succeed while others have failed miserably. If you are considering a capital campaign, here are some key items to consider:

### 1. Hire a consultant

Very few capital campaigns are done well without a consultant. People often say, "Consultants are too expensive." We believe that it will be too expensive to not have a consultant. When leading a campaign, you have one opportunity to make the big ask. Don't miss your opportunity because you didn't want to pay money to a capital campaign expert. Consultants consistently raise more money than self-led campaigns. Suppose you are embarking on a $1 million campaign and the consulting fee is $50,000. Many people will focus on the $50,000 dollar decision and fail to recognize that they are really making a $1 million dollar decision!

Most leaders have never led a capital campaign and can become intimidated by such a great task. A great consultant will be a trusted advisor throughout the preparation process and will help with the major ask. Be sure to hire a consultant that will also provide excellent follow-up to ensure that pledges are actually fulfilled.

## 2.  Think shorter vs. longer
It used to be the standard to ask for three-year pledges. We have seen that three-year campaigns are less effective in many church communities than one- or two-year campaigns. Shorter time periods allow you to accommodate changes that can happen swiftly – three years can be an eternity in a rapidly-growing church! An annual campaign is a great option if you are in a fast-growing church because it allows you to cast vision each year and engage those who are new to your community.

## 3.  One-time offering
Be sure to ask for a first-fruits offering at the beginning of a campaign. A lot can be done in one day when people sacrifice together! Plus, many of your larger donors are business leaders who clearly understand the importance of minimizing finance costs.

## 4.  Be clear
In order for people to give maximum gifts, their next step or steps must be crystal clear. A general ask for money will

yield a general amount. A clearly outlined and specific ask will receive a more specific commitment.

## 5. Know people will leave

People leave churches during campaigns. This is just a reality. You are asking for people to give some of their treasure, and they might not agree with the next step. They might not be managing their money well. Whatever the instance, people will leave. Hiring a consultant can help you cast vision in a way that will minimize these losses.

## 6. Take your time

Do not rush your capital campaign. Provide at least six months of lead time before the public phase. This will allow you to accomplish critical behind-the-scenes work like meeting with high-capacity donors, clarifying the vision and answering key questions. This will help people receive the campaign better. Also, more than 90-percent of people's net worth is not in liquid form like cash. Most of their net worth is tied up in land, real estate or businesses. It takes time to sell these possessions and have the money ready to give.

## 7. Follow-up

Too many churches receive a commitment that fails to materialize into an actual monetary gift. A proper follow-up plan is crucial. You cannot spend a pledge card. Annual updates are certainly not enough. Be sure to update people on a frequent basis to show them how their money is making a difference.

One more thing – Be careful not to burn your people out by asking for huge gifts all the time.

# • 16 •

## *Learn How To Say, "No!"*

A leader who lacks financial confidence can find it difficult to tell a staff member that a program will not be funded. Without financial confidence, it can be difficult to tell the largest giver that their "directed gift" will not be accepted if they do not give it as an "unrestricted gift."

A financially confident leader with a strong vision can make tough financial decisions much more easily. Strong vision should guide every single decision. Vision will answer most questions before they are even asked.

This means that you will have to say, "No!" to great ideas. Clear vision will help you know that you are making the right decision. Understand that you are not telling the individual that their thought is a bad idea, but that it is simply not part of the vision.

A person might have an idea to start a school through your church. Christian education is a great idea, but it can wreak havoc on the primary work you are called to accomplish if it is not part of the vision. Tell the person that it is a great idea but not part of the vision God has provided you. This might not be popular, but it is the right thing to do. God has given you the vision to accomplish what He has called you to do – not what He is calling others to do.

# • 17 •
## Seek God's Direction For All Decisions

You will not have financial confidence if you do not seek God. You will have zero confidence in anything without God's direction and leading. Seek Him.

People might respond to your own ideas, but it will result in nothing of eternal significance if the ideas are not God-led. Seek God often. Make time in your schedule to pray every day. Beg Him to provide direction and vision for your ministry. Invite Him to participate in your daily life including your family. Ask Him to discipline you.

You are the leader. You have been given a vision and call from God. He will provide direction every step of the way if you ask Him.

It is easy to become so busy doing ministry that He is left out of the equation. Do not let this happen. Do whatever it takes to keep Him in the leadership position of your life and ministry. Ask Him what you should do – then do it.

Jesus made time to connect with his Father. We should too.

# • 18 •

## *Stay Awhile*

It is hard for a church to become financially confident when the pastor leaves every two years. It is equally hard for a church to become financially confident when the pastor changes his mind every three months.

It takes time for most people to develop trust in a leader. Just because you have the title "Pastor" does not mean that everyone will immediately trust you. Trust is developed over time through your actions, your words and your leadership. When your actions, words and leadership are directed by God, He will provide the people and resources to ensure His Will is done.

There is power in staying power. A clear vision delivered by a committed leader who follows Christ's leading is unstoppable — and it will lead to financial confidence.

# • 19 •

## *Be OK When People Leave Because You Talk About Money*

Many financially insecure church leaders are scared to talk about money because they are fearful that people will become angry and leave. To put it more bluntly, they are scared that the big givers will leave.

Be confident! In Luke 18, Jesus met a well-meaning rich young ruler, and He spoke the most straight-forward, hard-hitting financial message ever! He said, "sell everything you have and give to the poor." (Luke 18:18 NIV) The rich young ruler became sad and as far as we know, did not follow through on Jesus' command.

Jesus had ultimate financial confidence. He delivered the truth despite the potential consequences. He knew that the Father owned it all and was in control. We have the same Father, and He is still in control.

People will leave your church. Some will leave frustrated, angry, confused and hurt. Every pastor has experienced this before, and it hurts. It hurts because you know that you have done exactly what God has told you to do – yet people still leave. You are fired up about your God-given call, and it hurts when others reject that and leave.

It's OK. Remember that you are not in control of every person. You know what God has called you to do and the vision He has given to you. You have been entrusted by God with this vision and passion, and nothing – even angry people – is to stand in its way. Many pastors become overly concerned with those who leave the church, and make statements like, "We need to close the back door." Perry Noble (senior pastor of NewSpring Church in Anderson, South Carolina – www.perrynoble.com) has said that Christ has called the church "a body," and if the body does not have a back door, it can become ugly very quickly! Recognize that when some people leave, it is a sign of a healthy church. Love each person – even as they leave. They are loved by God, and sometimes God uses Holy discontent to move people toward their next step.

# • **20** •

*Be A Generous Church*

Generous church leadership produces generous church membership. How much money does your church give away to entities outside your own ministry? We ask church members to give and sacrifice greatly, but many leaders struggle to do the same with the church budget.

Why should your church become a generous church?

**1. Jesus became poor so that we might become rich.**
Nothing else needs to be said. He gave everything.

**2. We can build the Kingdom faster**
For instance, investing $50,000 in a church plant might produce more Kingdom return than investing the same amount in a staff position.

### 3. Our people trust us more when we give.

If you consistently share stories of how your church is generously giving back to the community during your offering times and messages, don't you think people will trust your heart more than if you keep everything hush hush? People love to give to projects, ministries, churches and missions where they can see life change happening.

Here are some ideas on how you can become a generous church.

### 1. Start from the beginning

If you haven't started your church yet, allocate a percentage of your budget that you will give away from the very start. You will never miss it, and you will embed generosity into your church's DNA.

### 2. Start somewhere

Crosspoint Church in Nashville, Tennessee, (www.crosspointchurch.tv), has given away 10 percent of their budget from the very start. Their goal is to give away 20 percent, so they are giving away an additional 1 percent every year for the next 10 years to achieve it.

### 3. Start a tradition

Give away the weekly offering once each year on a specific Sunday. When churches do this, people respond with radical generosity that benefits the Kingdom. Balance faith and wisdom in this area. If the church will go bankrupt because you give your offering away this week, be sure it was God telling you to do it. It is much easier to do this when you have financial confidence because you have established financial margin!

Start today by giving something away.

# • 21 •
## *Celebrate The Vision*

God has given you strong vision. Do not apologize for it. When God burdens your heart with a call and clear vision, He will provide people who will help you accomplish it. It is important to celebrate the fact that God has chosen to use you and your church.

The Bible is filled with occasions where a landmark was built to celebrate a major event that occurred when God showed up and moved on behalf of His people. Be sure to celebrate the times that God has moved on your behalf. Share the vision that God gave you and tell the stories of life change that prove God's faithfulness. Tell the stories of how God cured disease, healed addictions, restored marriages, repaired broken relationships and delivered forgiveness. Celebrate baptisms and salvations.

Whenever you are faced with huge issues and you cannot see how God could possibly be at work, remember the past and how He has been faithful. God is faithful. He is true. Celebrate even more in times of struggle. You know that He will move greatly upon your behalf as long as you follow His lead.

Provide regular opportunities for the entire church to hear the life change stories. As the leader, you hear stories of life change all the time; your church community may not, and they need (and want) to hear them!

The stories of God's past faithfulness will lead to future confidence. This is essential when building financial confidence within your church and community!

# • 22 •

## Win With Your Own Money

If you are broke and mismanaging the resources God has entrusted to you personally, it is highly unlikely that others will trust you enough to give to the vision God has given you.

Spend less than you make. Invest for the future. Avoid outrageous debt. Give generously.

God's word is clear that we are to manage the resources He has provided us to the best of our ability. We should model generosity and give at least 10 percent, but we should never forget that He still owns the remaining 90 percent. It is our job to be the best manager possible of the resources He has provided — the 10 percent and the 90 percent.

Broke leaders find it difficult to preach what God's word says about money. It is impossible to tell others to give with over-the-top generosity when you are not doing so yourself.

If you are mismanaging your money, confess and repent. Seek financial counseling. Find a mentor who has won with money. Establish accountability.

God has provided enough. Live your financial life like you believe it.

# • **23** •

*Don't Hire Broke People*

If a person cannot manage his personal finances, it is doubtful that he will manage the church's finances well. Broke people bring stress and pressure to work with them. Proverbs 13:4 states that "the sluggard craves and gets nothing, but the desires of the diligent are fully satisfied." It is true. Those with nothing will crave everything. They are highly susceptible to believe that more stuff is the only answer to their financial issues. This will translate to excessive spending at work. Broke people are more likely to relentlessly ask for a raise because they believe more money is the answer to their financial woes.

It is clear that God cares about how we manage money. He cares that we tithe and give sacrificially. He also cares about the remaining money that He has entrusted us to manage. Check the giving records of each potential employee. If they are not givers, do not hire them!

As the leader, you are entrusted to manage God's money to maximize it for kingdom impact. Hiring a broke person to manage gifts given to God's work simply does not make sense!

Great interview questions to ask are:
- God challenges us to manage with excellence the financial resources He has provided. On a scale of 1 to 10, how well do you manage your personal finances according to God's Word?
- What are your thoughts regarding debt?
- Have you ever participated in a personal finance class?
- Are you winning with your money?

# • 24 •

## *Don't Hide Financial Mishaps*

Everyone has financial mishaps. No one is exempt. When you make one, address it openly and swiftly.

Financial mishaps appear in many forms. You may purchase land and later determine that this land does not help you accomplish the vision. Money could be invested in a new ministry that fails miserably. An error could be made by accounting. A member of your ministry team could spend more than the budgeted amount and as a result impact other ministry areas. A new piece of technology could be purchased and fail to deliver what was expected.

Ensure that you have built an open line of communication with your team. Tell them early and often that any and all financial issues must be communicated to you.

Do not provide a guarantee that there will be no consequences when someone commits a financial mistake. Some mistakes must be punished! Embezzlement, gross misappropriation of funds and theft are obviously grounds for immediate dismissal and possible prosecution.

The top barrier to maximum giving is unanswered questions. Financial mistakes will lead to questions – no matter how hard one tries to prevent their disclosure. In order for God's Kingdom to be fully funded, be ready to address financial mishaps forthrightly and honestly.

Implement an annual audit by an independent third-party to ensure that maximum accountability is in place. Audits cost money, but they will ensure financial mistakes are discovered and addressed. More importantly, it will minimize the potential for future mistakes.

# • **25** •

## *Don't Strap The Church With Outrageous Debt*

Debt is not a sin; however, obtaining debt is a decision that must be carefully considered and prayed about. Proverbs 22:7 says that "the borrower is servant to the lender." When a church is strapped with tremendous debt, it can prevent the vision God has given from becoming reality.

Debt is really the act of pledging away some of tomorrow's offering, some of next month's offering, some of next year's offering and possibly a decade of offerings.

Tremendous debt obligations restrict the use of money for ministry. The interest alone can rob your church's future potential.

When considering debt, ask yourself the following questions.
- Do we really need this?

- What other options are available?
- If we agree to borrow money, do we have a detailed plan to pay it back?
- Is this what God wants us to do?

Outrageous debt has caused many strong churches to stumble or fail completely. A good guideline is to never acquire debt more than one year's tithes and offerings. Definitely do not acquire debt that exceeds two year's tithes and offerings.

Less debt equals more financial confidence.

## **26**

### *Get Away Often*

Make it a point to get away often. Block out one workday a month to work off-site at a place where you will not be interrupted. Take care of the mundane detailed work that you need to do, but will never get done if you are in the office.

Go on vacation with your family regularly. Eliminate the distractions – including the cell phone and laptop. Go somewhere that is culturally and geographically different. You might have heard it said that a "change of place plus a change of pace equals a change of perspective." It is true.

Learn something new. Take dance lessons with your spouse. Participate in a cattle round-up. Help build a home with Habitat For Humanity.

Jesus often went away from the crowds. From Scripture, it is clear that He was closest to His Father during those times. He heard from the Father regularly. While He did not always hear what He wanted, Jesus obtained the strength to face the future during His time away.

It does not matter where you go to get away, but get away.

# • 27 •

## "It" Is A Wasteland That Eats Cash

Everyone has an "it" that eats cash. It might be your creative artists who demand computers that cost three times more than a normal computer but do not deliver real additional value. Just say, "No!"

It might be a program that was effective in the past, but now it is a drain on the finances. Multiple attempts to resuscitate it have failed. Just say, "No!" A successful past is not justification for funding an unsuccessful future.

Many times "it" is happening under the church's radar. This can be prevented by regularly reviewing the financial statements. Demand accountability for every dollar spent. This is not micro-managing – it is ensuring that the resources God has provided are being maximized for ministry.

Examples include schools that are bleeding cash and robbing the church to cover the school's operating budget.

Information technology departments are insatiable beasts that, left unchecked, can consume cash at unbelievable rates.

Other examples include underperforming staff members, legacy programs that no one participates in, and excess purchases of materials that will never be used. Wasted money equals missed opportunities for ministry and can lead to a lack of financial confidence.

Many leaders make the mistake of solely focusing on the large budget items using the 80-20 rule and focus solely on the largest items which account for 80 percent of spending. Be sure to focus on the smaller items as well – quarters, dimes, nickels, and pennies add up to dollars.

If "it" is not effective, eliminate it.

# • **28** •

*Pay Your Staff Well*

A well-compensated team exudes financial confidence. They operate from a position of plenty instead of a position of scarcity.

One of the number one ways you can communicate to your staff that you appreciate them and their work is to pay them well. If you cannot afford to pay a staff member a fair wage, then do not hire them without a specific plan to bring them to a fair wage. Passion and vision will only be able to sustain a person for a short time when the pay is not adequate. It is difficult for your employee to be passionate about your vision if they are unable to cover their living costs.

A staff that is paid well will be able to focus on ministry and use the skills, talents and abilities that God has given them without stressing about providing for daily necessities. A staff that is not paid well will seek ways to supplement their income and can become distracted from their daily duties in the pursuit of additional money.

God has given you plans, hopes and dreams. He will provide the resources for you to accomplish them. Be sure to remember that your team also has plans, hopes and dreams. You have the potential to help them meet many of them by paying each one of them well.

# • **29** •

## *Provide On-Ramps To Giving*

It is important to provide avenues for people to begin giving to your church. An offering plate is one way for people to give, but there are many other ways you can help them begin giving.

Establish online giving through the church website. Most people now pay at least one bill online every month. On-line giving with the ability for people to set up automatic recurring gifts is even better. As mentioned earlier, on-line givers who have set up automatic recurring gifts are the most consistent givers.

Challenge people to tithe for at least 90 days. Have them write down their commitment and include a reason why they are making the commitment. Ninety days is long enough to establish a new habit of intentional generosity!

Follow up with every first-time and second-time gift. Let them know how grateful you are that they have chosen to financially support the vision God has given you. Share stories of life change that have taken place as a result of those who have given to your church.

Provide giving envelopes with pre-paid postage.

If your church has a membership class, teach them the various ways that they can give.

Take advantage of community service programs available through local grocery stores. They exist throughout the nation and are linked to preferred customer cards. Each time a purchase is made using the preferred customer card, a portion of the purchase is donated to your church.

# • **30** •

*Budget Using Wisdom And Faith*

Many leaders follow a kind of doctrine that if we just have faith, the money will follow. While this might come true in some cases, it is not wise to budget based on a miracle every year. We have not found a scripture where faith and money are included in the same sentence. However, there are many verses where money and wisdom are highly connected.

Create budget projections using past results instead of future hopes and dreams.

If your church is just getting started, use extremely low projections.

When budgeting,
## 1. **Be simple**
Create a budget that people can actually understand. Don't let the super-duper smart guy create the budget

without first asking a non-financial person if they can understand it.

## 2. Be specific

The miscellaneous category should be small. Moving to a specific budget vs. general budget will feel like you gave your church a raise!

## 3. Be accountable

If you are exerting the time and effort to create a budget, ensure that it is followed! Establish monthly reports and quarterly reviews with staff teams to maintain accountability.

Budgeting well today will help you fund your next step tomorrow.

# • 31 •

## *Communicate With First-Time Givers*

First-time givers are special people. When anyone gives money to your church, they have made a spiritual decision. The magnitude of this decision is huge in people's lives. Jesus said, "Where your treasure is, your heart will follow." Whether their first gift is a tip or a tithe, communicating with these people is a great idea.

If you don't communicate, you are communicating. There are unintended consequences to someone who gives a gift and hears nothing. Most churches communicate when people sign up for a small group, volunteer team and baptism. We must do the same thing when they give. It is a big deal!

You can send a form letter, but we recommend a hand written thank you note. Handwritten notes communicate care and importance. Start this process today, you will not regret it.

# • 32 •

## Be Yourself

Pastors who see their vision funded are pastors who know who they are. Find your strength zone and live in it. We see the following types of leaders most often.

### The Preacher

If you are a preacher, then PREACH! When it comes to funding the church's vision, leverage your weekend sermons to help people hear God's heart on money.

### The Relational Leader

If you excel with relationships, be sure you spend relational time with high-capacity ministry and giving leaders. We suggest you invite people into your living room in groups of no more than 20 and share your vision with them for the next ministry step. Show them how they can participate financially.

## The Empowering Leader

If you love to see others win and want to increase their leadership capacity, discover the environment they thrive in and provide them opportunities to share their vision for generosity with those they lead.

What are your top three strengths?
(What gives you the most energy)

1. _____

2. _____

3. _____

How and where can you start sharing the church's vision in a way that leverages your strengths?

_____

_____

_____

_____

# • **33** •

## *Ask: Do We Really Need This?*

Every spending decision is a big decision. As leaders, we have to continually ask the question, "Do we really need this?" The sad reality in many churches is that church leaders spend money like it will always be there. Many churches struggle financially, and many times it is not because of income.

Nothing will decrease frivolous spending like a church spending system. Everyone on the team should be trained to understand that having a budget means they must operate according to the budget! Create a plan today that reflects God's heart for the wise use of the resources He has provided. The key to solving the question, "Do we really need this?" comes *before* the month begins not *after*.

# • 34 •

*Teach Practical Personal Financial Management Skills*

How many personal finance classes did you have in high school? If you have attended college, how many personal finances classes did you attend? The answer is usually one or none. There is a huge lack of knowledge in the world regarding personal finances.

We have seen that the personal financial condition of most church communities is no different than the community at large. This should not be! The Bible is FULL of wisdom as it pertains to how we should manage our personal finances. There are more scriptures about money and possessions than nearly any other subject in the Bible. God knows the important role that money can play in our lives.

If people are broke, it is extremely difficult for them to give generously and consistently. For you to build a financially confident church, you must teach practical personal financial management skills. Start by managing your own personal finances well. Share with your church how God's Word has impacted your finances. Teach the importance of giving, saving and spending the rest with a plan. Teach them that God owns all of our money; and we are just managers. Teach them the parable of the talents (Matthew 25). Offer classes on budgeting, debt elimination, saving for the future, investing and planning.

As you are teaching these practical principles, be sure to connect it to your church's vision. Show them how their obedience in managing their personal finances will allow God's vision for your church to be funded.

The schools are not teaching it. People are desperate for financial help. God's Word says a lot about it. Teach it.

# • 35 •

## *Provide One-on-One Financial Counseling*

A financially confident leader goes further faster when he has a financially confident congregation.

Everyone in your church family has money. Many of them deal with money struggles. This is also true for most of your surrounding community. Teaching Biblical principles about financial management can be a primary avenue for evangelism in your church, and it is essential for building a culture of financial confidence.

Most people struggle with their personal finances for one of two primary reasons: lack of education or lack of discipline. By providing free one-on-one financial coaching to individuals in your church and community, you are communicating that you care about way more than how much each person can give. You are communicating that you want each of them to win with his or her resources by applying God's Word and His Principles to all of their finances.

Challenge those in your church who have won with their resources to become financial coaches. After all, they are living witnesses to the fact that God's Word is true, and they will communicate this fact both directly and indirectly to those receiving help. These financial coaches exude financial confidence.

When people are helped in such a practical way as free financial coaching, it provides the opportunity to point them to Christ – the ultimate provider of hope and confidence!

# • 36 •

*Haste Makes Waste*

As leaders, we crave progress. This is a good thing, but be careful that you don't jump too quickly into initiatives that seem like a good deal but haven't been carefully thought through. Church planters are especially vulnerable to becoming intoxicated with their vision and end up making poor financial decisions. Sometimes it pays to just slow down.

The biggest mistakes are often made on incurring new fixed expenses. If you are hiring staff, increasing facility cost, or taking on a significant lease or purchase ensure that you understand the decision's impact on cash flow. Be extremely careful about taking on fixed costs just before summer. Too many leaders drain their reserves by making quick decisions in low cash flow months. Lack of margin means reduced financial confidence.

Review your past large financial decisions. Do you tend to rush into financial decisions, or do you always take the time to thoroughly evaluate each one?

Most of the decisions we rush into are actually good things, they just might not be the right timing. Haste makes waste.

Proverbs 21:5 states that "The plans of the diligent lead to profit, as surely as haste leads to poverty." Take the time to thoroughly review each decision to understand its overall impact on vision and its financial consequences.

# • 37 •

*Hire Consultants*

Great churches understand the value of an outside perspective. Secure leaders often use consultants. Insecure leaders oftentimes will not. The more secure the leader, the less threatened they feel from an outside perspective.

Two reasons to hire a financial consultant:

## 1. One-shot situations

If you are in a situation where you have one opportunity to raise a significant amount of money, you should hire a consultant.

## 2. Stuck situations

Your ministry is structured to accomplish what it is already accomplishing. If you need to break through to a new level of financial increase, hire a consultant. One or two key learnings from a consultant can lead to a huge financial difference.

**5 qualities to look for in a financial consultant:**
**1. How many clients they have**

You don't want a consultant with too many clients or too few clients. Too many equals a lack of follow through. Too few might indicate that they may not be very effective.

**2. Relational connection**

It doesn't matter how much they know about a subject if you can't stand working with them. Look for someone with whom you can become friends, not just consult with professionally. This will lead to better results and a more enjoyable experience.

**3. References**

Call references, but ask for more. Ask for the names of clients they have helped achieve excellent results and names of clients who have achieved poor results. If they won't do that, don't hire them.

**4. Connected to a local church**

It is important that a consultant is actively involved in his own local church! Call his or her pastor. If the pastor doesn't know this person, be careful. Consulting with the local church should be a calling, not a job.

**5. Ability to fire at any time for any reason**

You should negotiate the ability to fire the consultant at any time for any reason. Negotiate "pay as you go" terms. In other words, ensure that they work for the money you are paying them.

Hiring a consultant can be just what you need to take your ministry and team to the next level.

# • 38 •

*Know The Important Financial Numbers*

It is IMPERATIVE that the church's leaders know the church's numbers. Financial numbers are indicators of church health. Have a financial dashboard that allows you and your team to quickly gain a great perspective on your church's overall financial health.

Every church leader should know these numbers:

## 1. Income

Know weekly how much was given and whether or not this met budgeted needs.

## 2. Expenses

The leadership should know the big picture of how the church is performing according to the budget. A healthy spending system will control expenses.

### 3. Per Person Giving

Divide your weekly offering by your total attendance (every man, woman and child). If your church offerings last week were $7,500 and 475 people were in attendance, your giving per person would be $15.79.

This number is vitally important in measuring if your people are growing in their commitment toward biblical generosity. It will also help you in forecasting future budgets.

### 4. Attendance

You must know how many people are attending your church every week. It is the basic measure of ministry effectiveness. Numbers are important! God even gave us a book in the Bible called Numbers!

### 5. Digital Giving

How much money is being given via the web or through giving kiosks? If you don't have a strong digital giving presence, chances are that you are missing out on money that could be given to your church.

### 6. First-Time Givers

This is a great way to measure the growing spiritual health of your church. Money is one of the last things people will turn over to God. This measurement lets you know how many people are "signing up to give."

You can monitor additional metrics, but these are the fundamental financial numbers that need to be known and understood by your leadership team.

# • 39 •

## *Create A Staff Spending System*

Many lead pastors inadvertently become a lid on their church finances when they require that most purchases be approved by them. This approve-everything approach can consume enormous amounts of a leader's time, especially when the church is growing rapidly. To control spending and avoid having to say no all the time, create a spending system.

**Spending System**
1. Prepare a written church spending plan (a budget).
2. Divide the annual amount for each budget category into monthly amounts.
3. Assign responsibility for each budget item to a team member.
4. If they need to spend more than the amount budgeted, require approval from the person responsible for the overall budget.

5. Establish tough penalties if the budget is overspent without prior approval. For example, if they overspend their monthly amount, the overage will be deducted from their paycheck.
6. Require every person who spends money from the budget to turn in receipts with the appropriate budget codes written on them so that the expense is deducted from the proper budget line item.
7. Praise and reward people who are resourceful, and reprimand people who are wasteful. This is, after all, money that has been given to God's work!

It does not have to be difficult. Establish responsibility and establish consequences for both good and bad performance. It will work.

From experience, here are a few more tips regarding church spending systems.

- Do not have a church credit card that no one is responsible for; it will be overspent – often.
- Do not allow a volunteer to spend his or her own money and ask for reimbursement without gaining approval prior to the expenditure. This can lead to overspending and hurt feelings if not addressed appropriately.

A spending system allows the leader to have confidence that the money is being managed well. This allows the leader to focus on leading!

# • **40** •

## *Connect Life Change To Giving*

Nothing promotes financial confidence like people's lives being changed. A great strategy to get people to give more is to stop thinking and start praying for God to change people's lives radically in your church. Many churches connect giving to a building, a budget, a project, a program and many other tangible things. While this is a very good thing to do, it is important to NEVER forget to share with people the stories of lives that have been changed as a result of that project or effort. Buildings, projects, programs and budgets are simply tools that allow us to reach people for Jesus.

Communicate life change stories to your church often. Life change never gets old! When you baptize people, it is a perfect opportunity to share how giving has resulted in this person finding Jesus. Has a person been freed of drug or alcohol addiction because they met Jesus through your ministry? Ask him to share his story.

Was your church able to install a new playground at a local elementary school? Share the story and let the church community know that it happened because of their generosity!

Ask your team this question, "How can we communicate the story of people's lives being changed to our church?"

Life change fuels funding.

# • 41 •
## Connect Relationally With Your Church

John Maxwell says, "Everything rises and falls on leadership." This is true. We also believe that "Everything rises and falls on relationships." Relationships are a key reason that a lot of people give to a church. When people trust, they are more likely to give. Connecting relationally with your church in some strategic ways will help you finance the church's mission. Remember, the relationship must be the motive; but it would be naïve to think that generosity does not flow out of relational connections.

Ways to build trust with your church:
## 1. Blogging
A blog is a key way to build a relationship with people inside your church. Even if you are writing about random stuff, people will learn more about you and trust you more.

## 2. Twitter and Facebook

It is inspiring when a lead pastor shares something via Twitter that helps grow one's relationship with God and others. There is a connection when one hears about funny or crazy things occurring in that leader's life. These personal touches provide a relational connection with your church family.

## 3. Party at the Pastor's Home

Like it or not, people LOVE to come to the pastor's home. Create a summer tradition by having key ministry and giving leaders to your home. This special time will create a relational connection that is invaluable for building a sustainable and growing ministry. During these times together you can learn more about each person, pray and laugh together, remember good times and much more. All of this will build trust and pave the way for any request you might need to make in the future. Let these people be the first to hear news about the future. In other words, make them insiders to the vision God is giving you.

A donor's confidence in the leader leads to consistent giving.

# • **42** •

## *Maximize Year-End Giving*

People are more generous at the end of the year. As a church, it would be foolish not to maximize year-end giving. Every person in your congregation is being solicited for donations by hundreds of non-profit organizations. The church is one organization that Jesus said, "The gates of Hell will not prevail against it." The end of year giving season is a great opportunity to help people focus their gifts toward the Kingdom!

Here is a strategy to maximize year-end giving:
1. **Mail a letter to everyone the first week of November.**
      This letter should include a special year-end giving envelope. This envelope should be self addressed business reply mail. Ask people to consider what God would have them to give as a year-end offering.

**2. Send follow-up e-mail with link to online giving Web page.**

Create a Christmas-themed special year-end page for the church's website. Point people to the online giving portal.

**3. Mail a second letter accompanied by a vision letter.**

Include what will be accomplished through year-end giving. Again, include a self-addressed business reply mail special year-end offering envelope.

**4. Establish a date just before Christmas for year-end offering.**

Communicate this date to the entire church frequently.

**5. Issue a challenge during weekend services.**

State that your goal is for each person to give their largest gift this year to Jesus for Christmas – this provides perspective.

**6. Share a life change video one week before special offering.**

Share how Christmas brings out generosity in people.

**7. Week of offering, ask and ask big!**

People will provide – they want to!

Plan your year-end giving strategy in September. Don't miss your opportunity each year for this special giving season.

# • **43** •

## *Fix The Summer Slump*

Most churches see a decrease in giving during the summer months. This should be no surprise when it happens. Be proactive before the summer begins to help prevent the summer slump from affecting the ministry.

One key way to prepare for the summer months is to move as many givers as possible toward online giving. A few weeks after Easter, launch an online giving initiative.

**10 ideas for launching an online giving initiative**
1. Establish a goal for the number of families you want to start giving online.
2. Make sure your online giving system can manage recurring gifts, not just one-time gifts.
3. Name the initiative – something like "Consistent Generosity"
4. Create a funny video to illustrate giving online, and show it in your weekend services.

5. During announcement time, show people how to navigate to online giving on the church website.
6. Send out at least two different letters to your church attendees informing them about the website and explain how they can give online.
7. Buy giving kiosks for your lobby. (For example, www.securegive.com.)
8. Send e-mails to everyone in your church with a link to online giving.
9. Share stories of people who have moved to giving online.
10. Thank people who start giving online.

Because you make a big deal out of summer giving, people will respond. Don't just hope this year will be better than last year! Proactive is the key word to help with the summer slump.

# • **44** •

*Fund Life Change – Not The Squeaky Wheel*

Budgets should not be based on fairness. Budgeting should be based on ROI (Return on Investment). The greatest return on investment should get the most dollars. The return on investment is based on life change.

It would be ridiculous for us to tell you exactly what to fund because each church has a unique vision, but there is one thing we know to be true. Different ministry areas will ALWAYS want or think they need more money. The squeaky wheel is often a staff member who desires fairness in budgeting more than church priorities. We should look at these people as passionate leaders looking for funding – which is not a bad thing – but be sure that the loudest person is not the one who receives the most budget attention simply to appease them.

What do you spend the most on? Ask yourself WHY you are spending money on that item or program? Is it bringing the greatest return on investment? If there is no ROI, learn how to say, "No!"

# • **45** •

## *Model The Way – Be A Generous Giver*

Generous pastors/leaders produce generous churches. How much money do you personally give away? This is where the rubber meets the road! Where you give your money is where your heart is, period. This is why having your personal finances in order is very important as a leader. It will be very hard to ask people to do what you aren't willing to or can't do financially.

There are two prevailing mindsets when discussing personal generosity – abundance and scarcity.

Abundance = Give at any cost
Scarcity = Protect at all cost

Here are some questions to ask yourself:
- What is your first thought when asked to give?

- If you had to describe your church as a church of abundance or a church of scarcity, which most closely describes it?
- Do you get excited to receive all of the letters that arrive in the mail requesting money for summer mission trips?
- Would people around you say that generosity is a way of life for you?
- When is the last time you privately gave someone something that cost you a lot personally?

These questions are great ones to ask ourselves regularly. Personal generosity is not discussed often enough. As leaders, we must lead the way in generous living. If you are not living a generous life, start today by giving something away.

# • **46** •

## *Develop A Generosity Brand*

A generosity brand can be created to help people understand how to give, where to give, and why it is important to give.

Here are some examples of churches that have created generosity brands.

Mountain Lake Church in Cumming, Georgia, (www.mountainlakechurch.org) has created a generosity brand called Visionary Giving. Visionary Giving means "giving with a vision of your giving dollars equaling life change." People connect with this better than the generic term of "giving." MLC uses offering times, newsletters, and communication as opportunities to communicate the goal of Visionary Giving.

Granger Community Church in Granger, Indiana, (www.gccwired.com) has created a generosity brand called "Three Ways To Give." They have been very intentional about creating a brand that communicates how people can give: online, kiosk or in service.

What can you do to create a generosity brand in your church?

# • **47** •

## *Have A Mentor*

The book of Proverbs shares the importance of having wise counselors. Mentors can be extremely important in creating a financially confident church. When we surround ourselves with people that are further down the road than we are, success seems to come much more quickly. God is honored when we are surrounded by wise counselors.

This is a financial issue because the more a pastor meets with mentors, the more confidence the pastor has to live out the vision and mission of what God has called him to do. Hebrews 12:1 tells us "Therefore, since we are surrounded by such a great cloud of witnesses, let us throw off everything that hinders..." Who are the witnesses? Those who have been where you want to go! They are witnesses to the power of God working on their behalf and their confidence in what He has done in the past will provide the fuel for you to pursue what God has birthed in you!

Many people struggle with finding a strong mentor. If you know someone who would make a great mentor for you, ASK THEM. Rarely will someone walk up to you and say, "I want to mentor you." Mentoring is usually a result of someone wanting to grow. Mentors in our marriage, relationships, career and other important areas of life can generate tremendous confidence!

Who do you have in your life that you actually meet with on a consistent basis? If you do not have anyone, who can you ask?

Mentoring will take you and your church further faster!

# • **48** •

## *How To Ask People For Money*

Here are five ways to ask for money.

### 1. Ask in person

Letters and e-mails are great, but a lack of personal touch can make it very easy for the donor to say, "No." Looking someone in the eye and sharing your vision tends to generate buy-in and larger gifts.

### 2. Care about the person

When a person raising money talks only about "their deal" for the entire conversation, they will generally lose their audience. After all, this is all about working together to fund God's Kingdom.

### 3. Be simple

Complicated pro-formas are intimidating and mind-numbing. A donor doesn't need to know everything, and most don't want to know every detail. Too much information can distract the conversation from the key point – funding the next step!

## 4. Make the ASK!

You have to ask, "Will you support our church plant financially?" or "Can I count on your financial support for this next step?"

## 5. Meet with husband and wife

If you are meeting with a married couple, ask them together. According to Genesis 2:24, they are now one – a united team. There is great power in allowing them to experience the conversation together. It allows questions to be answered by both of them – which is key because the No. 1 barrier to maximum giving is unanswered questions!

# • **49** •

## *Prioritize Your Family*

You have a call on your life. It is strong, and it fires you up every day. You probably talk incessantly about it and have dedicated your life to fulfilling it.

It is great to have a tremendous burden and call placed on your life and very rewarding to fulfill that call. When this happens, however, you can be drawn to place everything and everyone into secondary roles – especially your family. Do not do this! At all costs, make sure that your family is first and KNOWS that they are first in your life.

Go home at a reasonable hour. When you are home, talk to your family. Make family time just that – family time. Do not schedule meetings, phone calls or visitation during that time. You are called to lead your church, but your most important call is to lead your family. You cannot do that well if you do not spend time with your spouse and children.

Take time out of your schedule to travel with your family. When you go on vacation, leave work behind. Turn the cell phone off. Unplug the computer. Better yet, leave it at home!

You will never feel financially confident if your family does not feel that they are first in your life.

# • **50** •

## *Talk To Non-Christians About Giving*

Many pastors have said, "You don't know our church. Most of our people are not even Christians yet. We kind of stay away from talking about giving because we don't want to run off non-Christians."

We point pastors who say this to the story of the Rich Young Ruler found in Luke 18:18-23. Observe how Jesus responded to the rich, lost man.

"When Jesus heard this, he said to him, 'You still lack one thing. Sell everything you have and give to the poor, and you will have treasure in heaven. Then come, follow me.'"

Jesus knew that this man had one hurdle in following – money. He made the "big ask" and the young ruler was "very sad." Jesus was very clear about what he wanted the man to do – "give [your money] to the poor."

What can we learn from this story?

1.  It is OK if people get offended when you talk about money —
    even when you bring it up right away!

2.  Talking about money will thin the herd (decrease
    attendance).

3.  Some people are addicted to money and can't fully follow
    Jesus until they give it away.

4.  Jesus cared more about this man's heart than his campaign.
    Notice Jesus didn't say, "Give your money to my deal." Jesus
    said, "Give your money to the poor." Motives matter.

5.  Jesus didn't say, "Well, I hate to talk with you about this, and
    you can do this if you want." He didn't apologize! If Jesus did
    not apologize for talking about money, you can quit
    apologizing, too.

# Continue the conversation!

Visit the Funded And Free website for additional resources.

**www.FundedAndFree.com**

THE
CHANGE
GROUP

Casey Graham is the founder of The Change Group an organization created "to help churches be Fully Funded and Financially Free." The Change Group fulfills their vision through providing:

1. **Virtual financial services to local churches**
   These services include virtual bookkeeping, payroll, audits, annual reviews, and tax planning for ministry leaders.

2. **On-site financial coaching**
   This service focuses on increasing operational revenue and general budget giving for local churches.

3. **Online resources**
   Simple digital products that help church leaders become fully funded and financially free.

Casey is a graduate of Samford University in Birmingham, Alabama, where he obtained a BS degree in Business Administration. While at Samford, Casey met his wife Kacie (yes, they have the same first name). They currently reside in Atlanta, Georgia and have one daughter, Darby.

www.TheChangeGroup.tv
www.BeanCreator.com
[877] 730-0854

# I Was Broke.
# Now I'm Not.

Joseph Sangl is the founder of I Was Broke. Now I'm Not., an organization that is passionate about "helping others accomplish far more than they ever thought possible." The IWBNIN team focuses on fulfilling their passion through workshops, public speaking, one-on-one financial coaching sessions, websites and financial articles.

Joe obtained a BS degree in Mechanical Engineering from Purdue University in 1996 and an MBA from Clemson University in 2001. From 1996 to 2006, he worked in corporate America for two Fortune 250 companies. During this time, Joe held engineering and management positions, but he developed a passion for helping others win with their money. In 2003, he began teaching personal finance courses and conducting one-on-one financial coaching sessions. In September 2006, he fired himself and embarked on a national crusade to help others with their finances.

Since that time, Joe and the IWBNIN team have taught tens of thousands of people. He has been featured in Money Magazine (the world's largest personal finance magazine) and writes a weekly newspaper business column called "Money Help". He is the author of two books: *I Was Broke. Now I'm Not.* and *What Everyone Should Know About Money Before They Enter The Real World*.

www.IWBNIN.com
www.JosephSangl.com
[864] 332-4151